SAMBA!

THE HEARTBEAT OF A COMMUNITY: AILTON NUNES'S MUSICAL JOURNEY

WRITTEN BY PHILIP HOELZEL AND ILLUSTRATED BY ANDRÉ CEOLIN

Published *by* SLEEPING BEAR PRESS™

IN THE MANGUEIRA NEIGHBORHOOD of Rio de Janeiro, Brazil, vibrant, joyful samba music filled the air. The unique mix of booms, clinks, bongs, and bangs always drew a crowd.

Every week the samba community met at the local samba school to spend time together and celebrate life.

Samba had been part of the community for many, many years, over generations. But samba was *more* than music. It was a way to honor the past and dream for a better future.

Mangueira was not a rich neighborhood. Not everyone had electricity, and candlelight illuminated many of the homes. The little money that residents earned was used first for food, next for shelter, and then for everything else.

But they had samba!

The highlight of the year was the annual spring Carnaval festival, especially the samba parades that were held in the huge Sambódromo stadium. Samba schools from all over Rio came to compete. Months before the actual event, Mangueira neighbors worked together to choose themes, write new theme songs, plan and build floats, and practice dance steps. The community made feathery dresses and costumes.

And the bateria—the drum section and beating heart of the show—would practice their percussion parts over and over late into the night.

From a very early age, Ailton Nunes couldn't stay away from the Mangueira samba school. Like a flower attracts bees, the sound of the drums attracted Ailton.

When he was about five, the local samba school lent Ailton's father a drum to play in the Carnaval parade. Many people in Mangueira could not afford their own instruments. Ailton's father let the young boy play the drum. Like the rhythm of waves crashing on Rio's beaches, Ailton pounded away on the instrument.

Sadly, after three days of playing, the drum had to be returned.

BANG. BOOM.

But not even the lack of a professional instrument would stop young Ailton. He and his friends made their own. Pots, pans, cans, and paper sacks from junk piles found new lives in the children's hands.

Ailton imagined joining the junior bateria of his samba school.

As Ailton grew older, instead of doing his homework after school, he could be found at the samba school watching and imitating the adults at their daily rehearsals. When he was lucky, the adults let him play, too.

He'd stand in his favorite position—right next to the drummers, feeling his heart thump to the pulse of the music. Ailton would close his eyes and imagine himself performing with the adult bateria.

The bateria director noticed Ailton's budding talent. He invited him to march next to them in the upcoming Carnaval parade. There was even a costume for Ailton to wear! He rushed home to share the news. For the first time, he could march alongside his parents.

But Ailton's mother said he could not go. He wasn't taking his schoolwork seriously, and missing Carnaval would be the consequence.

From then on, Ailton paid attention to his teachers and his studies.
He finished his assignments and asked for help when he needed it.
His mother watched him closely throughout the year.

Ailton, how was school?

*Ailton, are you finished
with your homework?*

Ailton, show me your report card.

Ailton nervously waited as the next
Carnaval parade approached.

His heart filled with pride when his
mother said yes! His dream had come true!
Ailton joined the youth bateria when
he was eleven years old.

Ailton loved playing at rehearsals, and then he would practice even more. He'd tap out beats on railings, boxes, and even on himself, drumming his way to another dream—joining the adult bateria at the age of thirteen!

Over the years, Ailton continued to improve. Within six years, he earned the role of first repinique—the high-pitched drum that starts and ends the samba songs.

When he was eighteen years old, Mangueira won its very first award for best bateria at the 1990 Carnaval! The community, the bateria, and Ailton celebrated their success.

Winning the award brought job opportunities. People and businesses wanted to hire the drummers, including Ailton. Ailton continued playing with the Mangueira group, but he also played onstage at a tourist location in Rio.

Eventually, Ailton left Mangueira. He spent ten years away, playing and teaching samba.

Over the years, while Ailton was gone, the Mangueira bateria got stuck in a long losing streak. Twenty years passed since they had won Best Bateria.

With just forty-five days before the 2011 Carnaval, the president of the samba school asked Ailton to come back and lead the bateria.

With such a short amount of time, his job wouldn't be easy.
Still, Ailton said yes!

As director of the bateria, Ailton formed a team of assistants to help coach more than two hundred musicians. At their first rehearsal, Ailton and his team asked the different instrument sections to play.

CLINK, CLONK, BA-BA-BOOM.

The drummers weren't playing together.

Ailton knew the bateria needed
to be more disciplined, just as
he had needed to be in school.

Together, Ailton, his team, and the drummers broke the music down into smaller parts. They mastered one section before adding another and another, until the entire piece was played. The drummers rehearsed the song over and over until it became natural.

Five times.
"That sounds better."

Ten times.
"Almost got it."

One hundred times.

"That's it! Ótimo!"

But being in sync wasn't the only challenge. Ailton needed everyone to sing the Mangueira theme song and march in time while playing their instruments. They also needed to invent exciting new dance moves as part of their marching. The competing baterias were very talented.

As Ailton looked out at the struggling musicians, he saw himself, too.

Mangueira wasn't a rich neighborhood, but its people were creative—just like he and his young drum-making friends had been. The bateria could win, but only if everyone worked hard, honored their talents, and dreamed big.

Could they do it?

On Carnaval day, the Sambódromo filled with thousands of people. Everyone was watching and waiting.

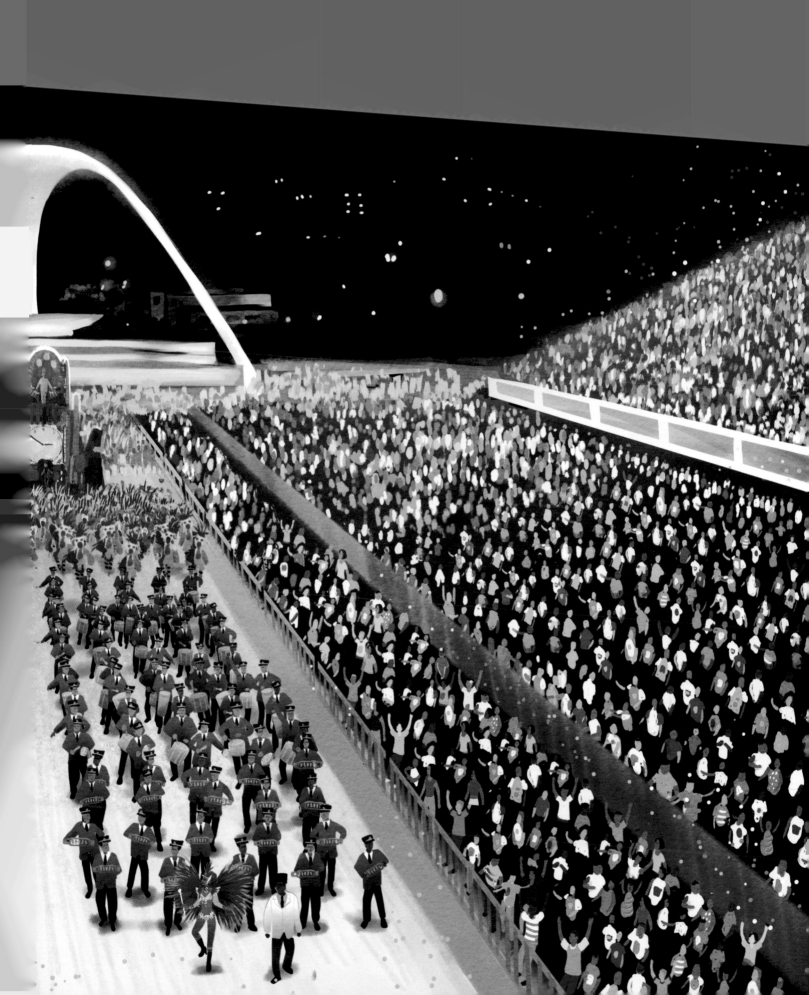

With sweaty hands and butterflies in their stomachs, Mangueira's bateria took their turn. Ailton blew his whistle and the bateria made their grand entrance. There was no turning back.

BANG. BOOM. BANG. BOOM.

Beat by beat, step by step, Mangueira advanced through the Sambódromo.

Then—just as they'd practiced—Ailton signaled the bateria to stop playing their instruments.

They continued singing Mangueira's theme song while marching. The entire audience rose to its feet and sang along.

At that moment, the bateria's focus wasn't on fancy floats or feathery costumes. It was on the Mangueira community's love for *samba*: the joy and powerful music that brought everyone together.

Like the flip of a switch, the bateria roared back to life!

BOOM, BANG, BANG, BANG,
BANG, BANG, BANG, BANG.

When the judges' scores were added up, Mangueira's
bateria won first prize once again.

Their hard work had paid off!

Ailton and his team knew they'd accomplished much more than winning. The Mangueira bateria had inspired the next generation of drummers to dream big, too.

I was introduced to samba in 2005, when a friend invited me to join Austin Samba—a fun, supportive, and challenging music and dance group. It was started by a man named Dr. Robert "Jacare" Patterson. He wanted to replicate the sense of community he had felt at the samba schools in Brazil—a place where everyone belonged, supported one another, and worked toward common goals. As part of his efforts to help establish a samba school in Austin, Texas, Dr. Patterson invited samba mestres—experts in samba—to teach the drummers. That is how I met Mestre Ailton Nunes. As a trained teacher myself, I recognize how great Mestre Ailton is at teaching and how he could motivate drummers to do their best. Mestre Ailton is kind, humble, patient, hungry to keep learning, and expects everyone to work hard. I feel fortunate and honored to help him share his story and to introduce samba to you.

—P. H.

WHO IS AILTON NUNES?

Ailton Nunes was born in Mangueira, Rio de Janeiro, Brazil. As a child, he lived in a one-bedroom house where the bathroom was located outside. He and his two siblings slept on a bunk bed in the living room. When Ailton was growing up, his school and his neighborhood didn't have a local playground. Outside of school, Ailton could be found doing chores like fetching water for cooking at the local neighborhood pump. For fun, Ailton played soccer in the street. But more often he went to the samba school where his family have been members for more than 95 years. Now, Ailton can be found spending time with his family, worshiping God in his faith community, and, when not at home in Brazil, traveling the world spreading the joy of samba.

WHAT IS SAMBA?

Samba is a form of music unique to Brazil. It is thought to be a mix of different types of music from Europe and Africa. The mix happened in the late 1800s, when many Afro Brazilians moved from the state of Bahia to the Praça Onze neighborhood in Rio de Janeiro. People moved for three main reasons. A new law said children born to slaves were free, another law ended slavery, and the newly freed people wanted to find work. These new residents of Rio de Janeiro gathered in the backyards of local matriarchs to practice their religion, celebrate life, and play music. It was here that samba got its start. The first song formally recognized as samba was registered in 1916 under the name "Pelo Telefone." The song was the creation of a group of Afro Brazilians who were part of the backyard gatherings in Rio de Janeiro. It was a hit at the Carnaval celebration in 1917.

WHAT IS A SAMBA SCHOOL?

Samba schools are important hubs for their communities. In addition to being gathering spots to play music, dance, and prepare for Carnaval, modern samba schools help their neighborhoods in other ways. It varies from school to school, but services provided include childcare for working parents, schooling for children, skills classes, medical and dental assistance, ballet classes, and more. The first samba school was founded around 1928 and named Deixa Falar. The Mangueira samba school was founded shortly thereafter. Samba schools are thought to be called schools because the first one was located next to a school.

COMMON INSTRUMENTS PLAYED BY A BATERIA

Agogô: A handheld two-toned bell

Caixa: A small drum carried on a shoulder strap or by hand up near a person's cheek

Chocalho or ganza: A handheld shaker that uses small metal cymbals to make noise

Cuíca: A small handheld drum played by rubbing a stick attached to the underside of a drum head

Repinique or repique: A small drum carried on a shoulder strap. It is the drum that starts and ends the samba songs.

Surdo: A big round drum carried on a shoulder strap. There are typically three sizes of this drum. One size is called the first surdo, another called the second surdo, and the last one is called the third surdo. Each surdo has its own sound. In Mangueira, a different drum called the surdo mor is played instead of the second and third surdos.

Tamborim: A tiny handheld drum that is played with a flexible stick

Timbau: A type of hand drum carried on a strap